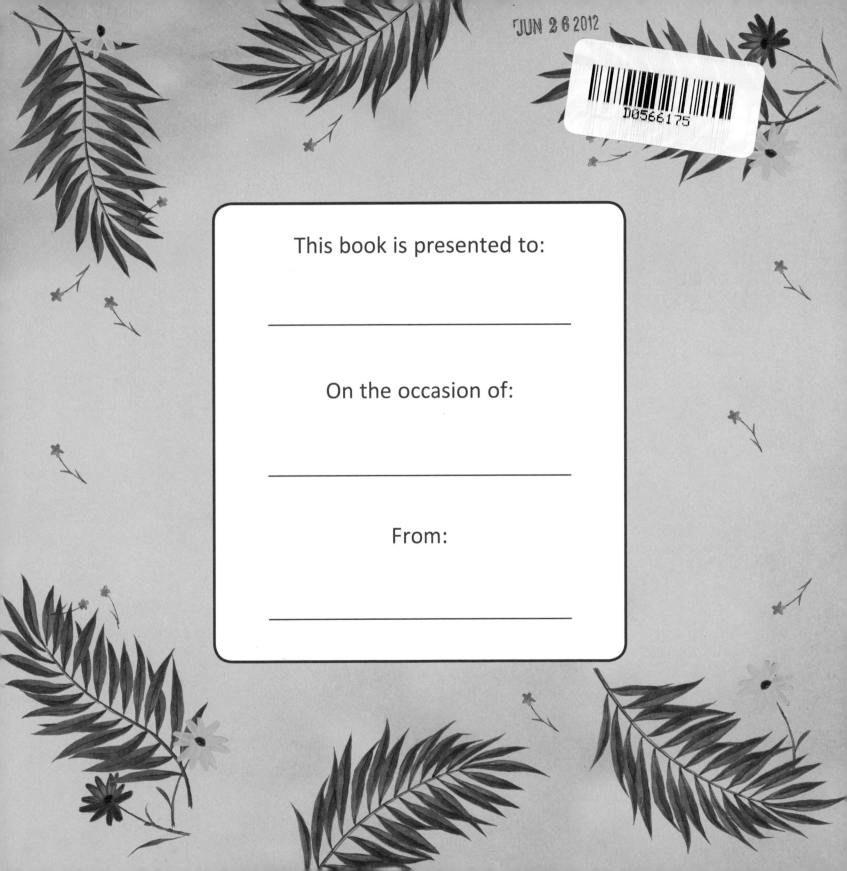

This book is presented to:

_____

On the occasion of:

_____

From:

_____

The Donkey That No One Could Ride

Anthony DeStefano
Illustrated by Richard Cowdrey

HARVEST HOUSE PUBLISHERS

EUGENE, OREGON

This book is for Bonnie and Jerry Horn.
–Anthony DeStefano

To the One who touched and changed my life. Hosanna!
–Richard Cowdrey

The Donkey That No One Could Ride

Text copyright © 2012 by Anthony DeStefano
Artwork copyright © 2012 by Richard Cowdrey

Published by Harvest House Publishers
Eugene, Oregon 97402
www.harvesthousepublishers.com

ISBN 978-0-7369-4851-7

For more information about Anthony DeStefano, please visit his website www.anthonydestefano.com.

Design by Mary pat Design, Westport, Connecticut

Printed in China

12 13 14 15 16 17 18 / LP / 10 9 8 7 6 5 4 3 2

Jesus went on toward Jerusalem…he sent two disciples ahead. "Go into that village over there," he told them. "As you enter it, you will see a young donkey tied there that no one has ever ridden. Untie it and bring it here." …So they brought the colt to Jesus and threw their garments over it for him to ride on. As he rode along, the crowds spread out their garments on the road ahead of him…all of his followers began to shout and sing as they walked along, praising God for all the wonderful miracles they had seen.

"Blessings on the King who comes in the name of the LORD!
Peace in heaven, and glory in highest heaven!"

LUKE 19:28-38

There once was a donkey—young, weak, and small,
So weak he could carry nothing at all.
Even when children sat on his hide,
He'd wobble and tumble and fall on his side.

No matter how much he tried or he cried,
This was a donkey that no one could ride.

He couldn't haul stones;
He couldn't dig ditches

Or carry rich men with their big bags of riches.

He couldn't pull carts
With huge bales of hay;
Just lifting a feather would make his legs sway.
No, this donkey was useless, no good at all,
Too puny, too shaky, too scrawny—too small.

Now the donkey's owner was quite mean and tough.
He said to the donkey, "I've had quite enough."
He pointed his finger and said with a huff,
"You can't lift a person,
No matter how light,
So take all your things
And get out of my sight!
Go away from here, Donkey.
Go away and just hide.
What use is a donkey
That no one can ride?"

So the donkey was led
To the far edge of town,
Pulled by his neck
With his head hanging down.
He was tied to a post on a small dusty road
And left all alone while his tears overflowed,
Left all alone and wondering why
He was born to be weak, and born to be shy,
And born to be frightened,
And born to cry.

Just then, two men appeared alongside
The post in the village where the donkey was tied.
They came without warning on that fateful day;
They came and untied him and took him away.
The donkey was frightened. He said to the men,
"Where are we going?" and then said again,
"Where are we going? And what about me?
Please leave me alone and just let me be!"

"Keep quiet!" the men said. "We mean you no harm.
Just follow us quickly, no cause for alarm."

They walked on for miles and miles until
They got to a town at the foot of a hill.

At the foot of the hill stood a man tall and thin,
Wearing a cloak and a beard on His chin.
He had eyes that seemed sad and longish dark hair
And a voice soft and gentle that floated on air.

He said to the donkey,
"It's time that you knew
About the great thing
That you're destined to do.
You'll carry Me into the city—we two.
Into the city, I'll ride atop you."

"What's that You say?" cried the donkey with dread.
"There's simply no way! You've been misled!
I'm just a small weakling. You must go ahead
And look for another to take you instead!"

"You see I'm just hopeless!
Ever since I was born,
I've been subject to insults and teasing and scorn."

"My back's somewhat crooked;
My legs aren't strong.
I'm just a big failure
who does everything wrong."

"Won't You believe me?"
The sad donkey cried.
"Just leave me alone and cast me aside.
I'm just a poor donkey that no one can ride."

The man looked at him with a face that was wise,
With a warm tender smile and love in His eyes.
And then in a calm and mysterious way,
He opened His mouth and started to say,

"My help is enough;
It's all that you need.
It's all you require in life to succeed.
The weaker you are,
The more strength I give.
I'll be there to help you
As long as you live.
I know you feel tired and frightened and broken,
But do you believe
These words that I've spoken?
Do you believe—I ask you again.
Do you have faith
I can heal you, my friend?"

For some reason the donkey was sure that he knew
The words the man spoke were honest and true.
They were said with such kindness and caring and love;
It seemed that they came from heaven above.
The donkey burst out, "I believe that it's true!
I believe," he repeated. "I believe, yes I do!"

The man stretched His hand out and closed both His eyes,
And then to the little donkey's surprise,
He felt a sensation he couldn't control—
From the top of his head right down to his soul.

All of a sudden, he realized that now
His body was stretching and changing somehow.
Most amazing of all, at that very hour,
The donkey began to sense he had POWER!
He didn't feel small or weak any longer.
Instead he felt stronger...and stronger...and stronger!

He could feel in his body the energy flowing;
He could see with his eyes that his muscles were growing.
His back felt like iron.
His legs felt like steel.
His chest felt so strong, it just couldn't be real!

"It's a miracle! A miracle!" the donkey cried out.
"A miracle! A miracle beyond any doubt!"

In order to show all the thanks that he felt,
The donkey bowed his head down and knelt
In front of the man who had made him so strong—
With a beard on His chin and hair that was long.

The man looked upon him with sorrowful eyes,
Then sat on his back, and told him to rise.
"We're bound for that city that's west of the hill.
I have a great mission I need to fulfill."

The donkey got up; his tears had all dried.
With big bulging muscles, he started to stride.
No longer a donkey that no one could ride,
Now he had courage and power and pride!

He started to stride; he started to run.
He couldn't believe he was having such fun!
With a clipity-clop and a clipity-clop,
He kept right on going with no need to stop.

But as they drew near to the gate of the town,
The donkey could hear a very strange sound.
The curious noise made him perk up his ears.
What could it be? *It sounded like...cheers!*

Soon crowds of people came into sight,
Shouting and waving their arms with delight.
They were cheering the man and giving Him praise,

Yelling hosannas and crying hoorays!
It was amazing to see the love they expressed;
They called Him a prophet and said He was blessed.

In front of the donkey, they threw with their arms
Flowers and garments and branches and palms.
They laid all these down and started to sing,
Calling the man a Savior and KING!

The donkey was happy—gone were his tears.
Never had people sung in his ears.
Never was there a moment so sweet
As carrying a king with palms at his feet!

And all his life after, the donkey rejoiced
That the King had made such a wonderful choice.
To help with the greatest mission of all,
The King used a donkey—
Young, weak, and small.

So every year at Easter time, renew YOUR hopes again!
Remember how a little faith can give YOU strength, and then
Gather all your friends around and tell the tale of when
A tiny donkey carried God
Into Jerusalem.